MARKET-BASED AND RIGHTS-BASED APPROACHES
TO THE INFORMAL ECONOMY

A COMPARATIVE ANALYSIS OF THE POLICY IMPLICATIONS

Antti Vainio

NORDISKA AFRIKAINSTITUTET 2012

NAI Policy Dialogue is a series of short reports on policy relevant issues concerning Africa today. Aimed at professionals working within aid agencies, ministries of foreign affairs, NGOs and media, these reports aim to inform the public debate and to generate input in the sphere of policymaking. The writers are researchers and scholars engaged in African issues from several disciplinary points of departure. Most have an institutional connection to the Nordic Africa Institute or its research networks. The reports are internally endorsed and reviewed externally.

Indexing terms
Informal sector
Hidden economy
Government policy
Development research
Research methods

Language checking: Peter Colenbrander
Cover photo: Ilda Lindell, *A market in Maputo*
ISSN 1104-8417
ISBN 978-91-7106-719-7
© The author and Nordiska Afrikainstitutet 2012
Production: Byrå 4
Print on demand, Lightning Source UK Ltd.

Contents

Abstract

This paper compares two different conceptualisations of the informal economy, a market-based approach and a rights-based approach. It reflects on the policy implications of a lack of consensus on understanding informal economic activities, and argues that the terms 'entrepreneur' and 'worker' are often ideologically charged rather than a reflection of the structural positions of the 'informals'. Moreover, the paper is critical of a market-based discourse and the related concept of informal entrepreneurs, as these may lead to policy recommendations that undermine the already fragile rights of people with informal livelihoods. The ideas presented in this paper are part of a work in progress and are meant to invite further debate about sustainable policy making that aims to enhance both the economic and social positions of people in the informal economy.

Foreword

Topics relating to informal economy have interested researchers and policy analysts for a long time and continue to be a source of lively debate. After decades of effort to reach consensus on a universal definition of the 'informal sector', research attention shifted towards understanding the processes driving informality and its locally embedded manifestations, though still with a pre-defined understanding of what constitutes informality. Others have come to question the usefulness or appropriateness of this notion for academic research and policy interventions, because of the many assumptions often associated with it. This Policy Dialogue belongs to a different analytical perspective that shows the continuing pertinence of talking about 'informality' – a perspective that seeks to understand how particular actors define and construct informality. The Policy Dialogue compares two different constructions of informality, one associated with the World Bank and the other espoused by an international advocacy network, each serving a very different agenda. Different assumptions and ideological foundations underlie their different understandings and definitions of informality as well as their different diagnoses of the causes of informality and of the problems requiring intervention. The policy prescriptions differ accordingly. Because such prescriptions impact people's daily lives, the examination of dominant constructions of informality as well as of alternative variants is an important academic endeavour.

This Policy Dialogue was written for the Urban Cluster of the Nordic Africa Institute in collaboration with the Department of Human Geography, Stockholm University.

Ilda Lindell
Associate Professor
Department of Human Geography
Stockholm University

1. Introduction

Since the informal sector/economy emerged as an area of interest in development research in the early 1970s, 'informality' has been used to describe a vast range of activities subject to relatively little or no state regulation. A plethora of approaches developed that differed in their explanations of causes, forms and consequences of informality, but no overarching definition of 'informal economy' is to be found.

> Given the prominence of the formal-informal dichotomy in the development discourse, one might expect to see a clear definition of the concepts, consistently applied across the whole range of theoretical, empirical, and policy analyses. We find no such thing. Instead it turns out that formal and informal are better thought of as metaphors that conjure up a mental picture of whatever the user has in mind at that particular time. (Guha-Khasnobis *et al.* 2006:2–3)

The dilemma of the informal sector has been framed as follows: 'Should the informal sector be promoted as a provider of employment and income, or should regulation and social protection be extended to it, thereby possibly reducing its capacity to provide jobs and incomes' (ILO 1991 quoted in Hansen and Vaa 2004). This question has been around since the informal sector was first 'discovered' in the 1970s, and still is a source of debate. Given the ambiguity of what is meant by 'informal economy', it can be argued that different definitions and conceptions can lead to different answers. Furthermore, different answers can be legitimised by the use of different conceptions of 'informal economy'.

The utility of the term 'informality' has also been a source of debate for a long time. I will not enter the debate about whether we should continue to use the term 'informal'. Perhaps its persistency should be taken as an indicator that it has descriptive value (Guha-Khasnobis *et al.* 2006:7). Some of the main academic approaches as well as the history of the concept of informal economy will be briefly surveyed below. The main aim of this paper is to move on to look at how different views of informality affect policy-making and intervention in the informal economy at different levels. By looking at how different conceptions of 'informality' relate to policy-making, we can see that how we understand 'informality' and the value that is placed upon informal economic activity have significant consequences for people in the informal economy.

I identify and compare two approaches evident in development discourse, a market-based approach and a rights-based approach. These two approaches are very broad and there are plenty of points of divergence within them.

7

However, the idea here is to identify some of the central characteristics of the two views and to analyse how they differ from each other. The market-based approach, inspired by Hernando De Soto, is mainly examined through publications of the World Bank. Analysis of the rights-based approach is mainly based on texts published by WIEGO (Women in Informal Employment Globalising and Organising) and its members, as well as recent academic literature. WIEGO was chosen because it is a very influential NGO in research relating to the informal economy and includes a wide network of researchers. It has been consulted for many UN reports and is often referred to in academic literature (ILO 2002, Chen *et al.* 2002, Lindell 2010).

I begin by briefly examining what the two approaches regard as informal, specifically who is regarded as being in the informal economy. Chapter 3 will then look at how the process of informalisation is understood and what factors are seen as contributing to increased informality. In chapter 4, the problems relating to informality are examined. While the market-based approach focuses on the economic effects of informality, stressing the negative effects on investment climate and thus on the welfare of the society, the rights-based approach focuses on social and political issues, advocating the rights of those in the informal economy. Poverty; lack of economic and social security; and inadequate opportunities for political participation are seen as the main problems to be addressed. Chapter 5 shows how the different conceptions of informality explored throughout the paper lead to different policy recommendations. The final chapter briefly examines the state and the informal economy, drawing on examples from sub-Saharan Africa. The aim is to look at how the market-based approach has influenced state policies, and the consequences this has had, as well as at how people in the informal economy may affect state policies.

This paper is somewhat critical of the market-based approach. It will be argued that the approach rests on a too narrow conception of informality, and that therefore the policy suggestions will not be relevant to the majority of those in the informal economy. The rights-based approach is examined as an alternative. Furthermore, it is argued that the use of a narrow conception of the informal economy may sometimes be intentional in order to justify a predetermined policy framework.

The market- and rights-based approaches should be understood as a somewhat simplified way of categorising different concepts of informality. No one text necessarily matches either of these categories perfectly, and there are variations within the approaches. The aim of this paper is to identify factors common to texts within approaches, in order to emphasise the contradictory nature of the different conceptions of informality. However, it should also be noted that the different approaches may in some aspects be complementary.

It has become typical in recent literature to state that the informal economy is hard to define and measure; that it means different things in different contexts; and that we should not think about the informal-formal relationship in terms of dualism (Potts 2008). The debate about why we persist in using the term 'informal', despite all its shortcomings, has also continued for decades. Yet relatively little research has seemingly been devoted to examining the policy implications of *how* the term 'informality' is understood and used. This paper aims to raise certain questions in this regard by comparing how the specific conceptions relate to policy recommendations.

History of the 'informal economy' concept and mainstream approaches to informality

In the 1950s and 1960s, colonial economies were thought to consist of modern and traditional sectors, the modern being characterised by efficiency and the Western bureaucratic model and the traditional by precapitalist modes of production, agriculture and inefficiency (Potts 2008: 152). It was assumed that with economic development, the traditional sector would disappear, or alternatively that in order for the economy to develop the traditional sector would have to disappear (Palmer 2004).

In the 1970s, the idea of 'informal sector' came to replace the modern-traditional dichotomy. It was noticed that the traditional sector was not disappearing, and that it displayed many 'modern' qualities. Keith Hart's fieldwork in Ghana followed by an International Labour Organisation (ILO) report on the informal economy recognised informal economic activities as having positive poverty-alleviating effects (ILO 1972, Hart 1973). During the 1970s, informality was seen to perform a function as a replacement for social security, a way for the poor to help themselves. Low technology was now seen as an advantage because it enabled involuntary growth, that is, production needed more labour and thus enhanced employment (Potts 2008:155). These early conceptions of the informal-formal relationship were essentially dualistic, because they ignored the links between formal and informal, and regarded the two as separate sectors.

A structuralist approach viewing the informal sector as subordinated to the formal economy emerged as a critique of dualism. The informal sector can be seen as keeping formal wages low by supplying surplus labour; working as social security for the poor in lieu of formal unemployment insurance; and by reducing costs of subsistence (Davies 1979:90-101, quoted in Palmer 2004). The structuralist view challenges the dualist notion of people in the informal sector as marginal or outside society. According to Castells (1989), these people are not marginal, but 'fully integrated into society, but on terms that often caused them to be economically exploited, politically repressed, socially stigmatised and culturally excluded' (quoted in Roy and Alsayyad 2004:9).

According to the legalist perspective, informality is a rational response to unreasonable costs of regulation (De Soto 1989). In terms of this view, those who run their businesses informally do so in order to increase their income. The legalist perspective is influenced by neoclassical economics, which holds that the economy needs minimal state intervention. For De Soto, the state should decrease regulation costs in order to increase formalisation. The role of the state is to protect property rights and legal order in order to allow free markets to promote economic development.

Of these broad views, the two last-mentioned ones are of greater significance here. The market-based approach is heavily influenced by De Soto. The rights-based approach, on the other hand, sees the structuralist and legalist approaches as too simplistic and emphasises the complexity of the informal economy (Chen 2006). Moreover, the rights-based approach can be seen as a critique of how earlier approaches ignore the political agency of people in the informal economy.

During the last decade, the term informal *sector* has been giving way to informal *economy*, in order to avoid dualistic conceptions of sectors and to promote a more complex understanding of informality (ILO 2002). Henceforward, I use the term 'informal economy', except when discussing a dualistic conception of 'informal sector'. In the interests of readability, the term 'informals' is used throughout interchangeably with 'people in the informal economy'. As will become evident, the term also has the advantage of obviating the use of 'informal workers' and 'informal entrepreneurs'.

2. What is informality?

Market-based approach

The market-based approach is here analysed mainly by looking at the *World Development Report 2005: Better Investment Climate for All* (World Bank 2004), as well as some of the research published by the World Bank. This market-based approach focuses on the impact of informality on the economy, the argument being that informality has an overall negative impact on the investment climate. Typically, this perspective emphasises the economic costs of informality, whereas the social and political aspects –positive and negative – are not seen as important.

This view is influenced by an enterprise-based definition of the informal economy, which is seen to comprise informal enterprises that evade regulation and taxation. Only those owning or working for informal enterprises are thus seen to be in the informal economy. Some of the studies even gather statistics about the size of the informal economy by equating informality with self-employment, and an informal firm with a person (Loyaza and Rigolini 2006). This definition was adopted in 1993 by the 15th International Conference of Labour Statisticians (ILO 1995). It is a view that tends to downplay linkages between formal and informal economies, seeing them as separate sectors. Informal economic activities are viewed as the opposite of formal; in competition with formal enterprises; and as *outside* the state. The focus has been on informal entrepreneurs who evade state regulation and compete with formal enterprises without contributing to state revenue. An altogether negative conception of informality is thus created.

Since the enterprise-based definition was first coined, it has been criticised as too simplistic and ignoring the heterogeneity of informal work arrangements (Chen *et al.* 2002, ILO 2002). Some of the literature advocating the market-based approach now recognises that the informal economy is more complex, but still makes policy recommendations based on the idea of informals as entrepreneurs (Oviedo *et al.* 2009, Kenyon 2007).

Rights-based approach

WIEGO recommends instead an employment-based definition of the informal economy. This 'would include all-non standard wage workers who work without minimum wage, assured work, or benefits, whether they work for formal or informal firms' (Carr and Chen 2002: 4). It is emphasised that people in the informal economy are not only employees, but include employers and self-employed. The informal economy is conceptualised as very broad and heterogeneous, covering a range of labour relations and work situations.

> The informal economy is highly segmented by location of work, sector of the economy and status of employment and, across these segments, by social group and gender. But most workers in the informal economy share one thing in common – the lack of formal recognition and protection. (Chen 2003:1–2)

This approach to informality is also to a large extent advocated by ILO, as indicated by the extension of the decent work agenda to cover the informal economy (ILO 2002).

The focus on heterogeneity and complexity within the informal economy undermines the usefulness of the informal-formal dichotomy. There can be different degrees of informality, and in practice most 'informal' activities fall under some form of state regulation (Pratt 2006). The informal and formal economies are not seen as separate sectors, but as part of the same continuum. 'Depending on their circumstances, workers and units are known to move with varying ease and speed along the continuum and/ or operate simultaneously at different points on the continuum' (Chen 2006:77). Examples include people producing informally for a formal firm; formal workers with an informal job on the side; and formal firms that use informal distribution channels. These examples emphasise the dynamic relationship between the informal and formal economies. ILO sees the challenge as moving greater numbers of workers towards the formal end of the continuum (ILO 2002).

Roy and Alsayyad make some interesting points about what informality is by arguing that it is an 'organizing urban logic [that] is not new, but made novel by the relation to globalization and privatization' (2004:5). These novel characteristics of informality mean that people may simultaneously belong to the informal and formal, and that informality is not limited to the poor: informal processes also spread across the formal middle classes and public sector workers. An interesting example is informal vendors who have an official distribution contract with Coca-Cola or Unilever (Chen *et al.* 2002:17). Thus, informal and formal economies coexist in a relationship that is not solely one of competition, but also includes constant movement of goods and people. Many products regarded as formal have at some point been affected by informal production or distribution channels. Similarly, the relationship between the state and informal economy cannot be reduced to one of opposition. The ways in which the state planning apparatus is producing the 'unplannable' should be considered. 'State power is reproduced through the capacity to construct and reconstruct categories of legitimacy and illegitimacy' (Roy 2005:150).

3. Causes of informality

Market-based approach

In looking at the root causes of informality, the market-based approach compares two explanations, 'exit' and 'exclusion'. 'Exit' means an active decision by a person to gain his/her income informally, whereas 'exclusion' refers to a situation where a person has no possibility of working within the formal economy and is thus forced to work informally (Oviedo *et al.* 2009). The enterprise-based conception of informality, with its focus on entrepreneurs, applies a notion of individual agency to people in the informal economy. 'Exit' is then seen as a rational choice to evade the regulatory costs of formality by running an enterprise informally and as a more important cause than exclusion. According to World Bank research, while exclusion is an important factor, there is 'growing evidence that a large share of formal sector workers choose to quit their job to become self-employed or salaried in an informal business' (Oviedo *et al.* 2009:3).

The reason for informalisation, according to the market-based approach, is that too expensive regulation makes running a formal business a luxury that the poor cannot afford (World Bank 2004, Loyaza and Rigolini 2006, Oviedo *et al.* 2009). Heavy tax burdens, restrictive labour market regulations and poor enforcement are listed as causes (Batini *et al.*, 2010). The problems can arise from excessive regulation, poorly planned regulation, poorly executed regulation, etc. A critical factor is also the perceptions people have of the advantages of formality, and whether or not they see taxes as contributing to their own greater good. What is noteworthy is the emphasis on the role of the state in creating the conditions for informalisation and on how the people in the informal economy are made active agents in the process of informalisation. As a result, a binary opposition is created between the bureaucracy (the state) and the people (informal economy) (Hart 2008). Informal economy becomes a symptom of bad governance.

Here it would be useful to explore the reasons people choose to quit formal jobs in the first place to become entrepreneurs. Then, the kinds of factors leading to a situation where informality is seen as the best alternative should be examined. When using notions such as 'exit', 'rational choice' and 'entrepreneur', we should be aware of the values attached to these words. All of them emphasise the role of the individual in the process of informalisation, diverting attention from the broader social processes that influence such decisions.

If one of the main reasons for workers exiting the formal economy is that shrinking wages no longer allow them to support themselves formally, can this situation really be said to be an example of 'exit'? In this case, the worker has to quit a formal job (exit) – or at least get an informal job on the side – as opposed to losing the job (exclusion). Perhaps the economic conception of informality is simply based on lack of understanding of the local dynamics in the informal economy. People are seen as having the luxury of making choices between registering their business and remaining informal, when in fact very often these choices are based on a need to survive.

Emphasis on the role of local factors in encouraging informalisation brings national governments into focus. This can be useful when thinking about the complex relationship between state and informal economy, because it brings home the point that the state should be associated not only with processes of formalisation but that we should also think about how state policies affect informalisation. However, if informalisation is only accounted as bad policy, something is missing from the analysis. Governments of developing countries do not act in a vacuum, but often react in their policies to broader global and local processes. In many cases, informalisation is linked to the structural adjustment policies of the 1980s and 1990s (Baah-Boateng 2007). These, while implemented by national governments, were among the conditions for World Bank loans and cannot be seen merely as a national policy issue.

Rights-based approach

Carr and Chen (2002) identify three main causes for the continuing expansion and growth of the informal economy. Patterns of economic growth mean that fewer formal jobs are being created. This may be due to lack of economic growth or because of capital intensive growth, so that the economy can expand without more jobs being created. Second, downsizing of the public sector as a result of neoliberal restructuring has pushed people into the informal economy. This is often linked to the structural adjustment programmes advocated by the World Bank since the 1980s. A third set of reasons is linked to globalisation and the world economy, because 'global trade and investment patterns tend to privilege capital … and disadvantage labour' (Carr and Chen 2002:2). Increased global competition as well as mobility of production are forcing large companies to move production to locations with low costs, as well as encouraging outsourcing to informal firms and the casualisation of labour. Many large formal companies are only focusing on core business and outsourcing their production, thereby becoming 'hollow organisations' (Klein

2000). Subcontracting chains can be difficult to trace and are often linked to informal production (Merk 2008). Furthermore, informalisation is complicated by how trade liberalisation is affecting the state's ability to provide social security. 'One estimate is that as much as one third of total tax revenue may have been lost in many countries as a result of trade liberalization' (DAW 1999, quoted in Carr and Chen 2002:8).

A comparison of these explanations with the market-based approach reveals a clear point of divergence in the understanding of the relationship between globalisation and informality. The market-based approach sees informalisation as a problem relating to national legislation and negatively affecting a state's potential to gain from participation in global markets. By contrast, the rights-based approach emphasises economic globalisation's role as a cause of informalisation, linking informalisation to the same processes that drive modernisation. For the market-based approach, trade liberalisation is a proposed solution to informalisation, whereas for others it is a cause. Fernandez-Kelly argues that informal economic activity is not a relic of the past 'but a by-product of advanced forms of production' (2006: 4). Urbanisation, industrialisation and the current form of economic globalisation are the driving forces behind increased informalisation. However, while the links between informal and formal in the form of subcontracting arrangements can be seen in negative terms as 'downgrading labour', it should also be acknowledged that these connections may also be spreading opportunity (Potts 2008, Chen 2005).

These different understandings of the causes of informality can be tied to different understandings of who is in the informal economy. The focus on informal enterprises ignores the informal work arrangements of formal companies and therefore does not necessarily capture that specific link between economic globalisation and informalisation.

4. Problems with informality

Market-based approach

According to the market-based approach, informality has negative effects for informal enterprises, formal enterprises and the state. Low profitability, low productivity and little growth potential are mentioned as reasons for promoting formalisation. Informal enterprises face challenges that hinder their prospects for development, including 'insecure property rights, corruption, policy unpredictability and limited access to finance and public services' (World Bank 2004:3). Informal enterprises are portrayed as being caught in an informality trap and incapable of enhancing real economic growth. However, because informal enterprises evade regulation costs, they have unfair advantages compared to formal firms. The informal economy is thus seen as somewhat parasitic, not contributing to society, and taking away business from those complying with state regulation. A large informal sector is also associated with lower GDP (Oviedo *et al.* 2009). Tax avoidance has negative effects for the welfare of the entire society because of lost state revenue. 'If some of these firms have the potential to grow, but lack the means, the economy as a whole loses if they remain informal and are unable to exploit this potential' (Oviedo *et al.* 2009:33). As a result, informality can be said to have an overall negative impact on the investment climate, thereby undermining the society's chances of successfully participating in the global economy (World Bank 2004).

There are a few problems with the argument based on these challenges and the negative impacts of informality for informal enterprises. On one hand, the argument is that informality is an advantage since informal enterprises save money by not paying expensive regulation costs. On the other, it is argued that informality is a burden that holds back these enterprises from increasing their productivity. It is argued that informal companies are prevented from developing by the disadvantages associated with informality, and that formal enterprises suffer by the unfair competition by informals. This argument takes two characteristics of informality – one of which has positive impacts for informal firms and negative for formal firms, and another of which has negative impacts for informal firms and vice versa – and only emphasises the negative impacts of both. If informality is hazardous for formal firms because it gives informal firms an 'unfair advantage', it has positive value for informal firms. It is not clear whether formalisation would help, since arguably it is precisely informality that keeps some of these enterprises going. As admitted by

Oviedo *et al.*, it is unclear 'whether these firms would survive as formal firms' (2009:33). It thus seems it is not actually possible to reduce informality to a positive or negative feature for informal firms. The advantages and disadvantages of informality should always be evaluated in a specific context.

The negative impact on formal firms is based on the assumption that the relationship between formal and informal firms is primarily one of competition. It is true that where there is competition between, for example, an informal street vendor and a formal supermarket, the street vendor possibly has an unfair advantage because she can have a larger profit margin due to fewer regulatory expenses. On the other hand, the formal supermarket can have the advantage of lower bulk prices. However, the relationship between formal and informal enterprises should not be reduced to competition, because this line of argument advocates a view of the two as separate sectors. As argued above, formal and informal economies are linked through chains of production, distribution and consumption. This point also highlights a shortcoming of the 'enterprise-based perspective' on informality, since it does not take into account the fact that formal firms are increasingly using informal work arrangements or outsourcing to informal firms as a way to cut expenses (ILO 2002). If the focus is not only on informal firms but also on the use of informal labour, the issue becomes much more complicated and we can see that many formal firms are at the heart of informalisation, reaping the benefits of informal labour arrangements.

A third set of problems with informality, according to the market-based approach, relates to the state. Informal firms that evade taxation and regulation are having a negative impact on state revenue (Kenyon 2007:4). This is a serious concern, but is more complex than may at first seem. Here the argument is that because of poor regulation, the state is losing income. However, the argument could be inverted: because of lost income, the state is no longer able to carry out effective regulation. State failure and informalisation should be seen as a sort of Catch-22, with each reinforcing the other. What needs to be addressed is the plethora of processes at work that are diminishing the state's ability to regulate its economy and to gain revenue. These processes cannot be adequately covered without also examining how global markets are affecting developing states, and how lack of regulation is motivated by global competitiveness.

There is also a link between how informality is seen as a threat to formal firms and how it affects the state. Since the public sectors of many developing countries were downsized as a result of structural adjustment policies, privatisation of formerly public services has played a major role in the market-led development advocated by the Bretton Woods institutions. Informality is now seen as a threat to this 'private sector development' (Hart 2008:18), which is often driven by global investments. This raises a series of moral questions about how specific forms of informality are seen in negative terms and others are ignored. Does the market-based approach seek to criminalise informality that is in competition with global investments, while ignoring informal work arrangements of multinational corporations?

Rights based approach

The rights-based approach tends to point out that informality *per se* is not a bad thing, but that, in fact, informal workers serve a purpose in society. The informal economy 'is a major provider of employment, goods and services for lower income groups. It contributes a major share of GDP' (Chen 2006:81). Neoliberal globalisation – especially structural adjustment programmes and trade liberalisation – have eroded the state, undermining its ability to fulfil all its functions. This is evident in the diminished public sector in many developing countries, as well as in the state's inability to provide infrastructure and services. Informal activities can then be seen as performing some of these functions while at the same time providing a safety net in terms of income for the poor. Waste pickers, for example, play a valuable role in regard to the urban environment, and street vendors provide goods for people who cannot afford the prices in formal markets (Bhowmik 2005, Wilson *et al.* 2006). Thus, the informal economy should not be seen in purely negative terms. The problem with informality is that people in the informal economy tend to earn less and lack social and economic security.

According to Chen (2003), there is a link between being poor and working informally, but this should not be equated with a causal relationship. The formal-informal continuum is characterised by different levels of poverty. Poverty increases as one moves 'from employer to self-employed to informal and casual wageworkers to industrial outworker' (Chen 2002:2). Women in the informal economy are generally worse off than men. The main challenge facing the informal economy is extending the rights that apply to people in the formal economy to those in the informal economy.

People in the informal economy are often prone to economic vulnerability. Lack of formal contracts means there is no security of future income, and limited access to financial resources means that informal firms are not able to handle even minor economic setbacks. And, because of the lack of social security systems, there is no alternative to informal incomes. Unemployment is not an option. Another problem is the exposure to political instability. Since legislation regarding the informal economy is often unclear, government attitudes are liable to fluctuate, with informal enterprises are often being blamed as a nuisance and for causing congestion, crime and disease (Lindell 2010). As a result, street vendors are occasionally cleared from the streets in 'clean up' operations, leading to losses of livelihood (Potts 2008). At the heart of this situation is the problem of inadequate political channels for people in the informal economy to participate in decision-making processes.

Some alternative academic approaches have recently also questioned the way in which informality is portrayed in development discourse. Cross and Morales (2007:9) are critical of 'a tendency to reify a formal category, retail trade, and diagnose problems with street markets or other residual activities as if it were a bad copy of the privileged category instead of appreciating them for what they are and what they can contribute.' We should abandon this 'formalomorphism' and understand informality in a local and historical context, so that development can occur where informal and formal economies have existed side by side. In a similar way, Roy argues that we should abandon the focus on First World 'models' and Third World 'problems'. The issue is that 'much of the urban growth of the 21st century is taking place in the developing world, but many of the theories of how cities function remain rooted in the developed world' (2005:147). A key contribution of these alternative approaches is that they point out that we should not see informality as a problem. We can look at the problems that exist within informality, but we should also identify how they are linked to the formal economy. Otherwise, we are left with a model that says that an informal street vendor is a problem, but a worker with no legal, economic or social protection working for a formal company is not.

5. Policy Recommendations

Market based approach

According to the market-based approach, the motivation for informalisation is regulation that makes formality too expensive. This leads to the conclusion that regulation should be made affordable so that firms will be more willing to formalise. Some of the policy recommendations include 'simplifying taxation schemes and reducing taxes on microfirms and small firms; reducing barriers to entry; allowing for more flexible hiring and firing of workers' (Oviedo et al. 2009:31). Priorities also include securing property rights and improving access to microfinance (World Bank 2004). In general, the main focus is on promoting economic liberalisation in order to encourage informal firms to formalise.

While the discourse concentrates on 'formalisation' of informal enterprises, there is also a recognition that many informal enterprises would not survive as formal enterprises. 'Instead, an efficient reallocation of factors would have labour and capital from these firms shifted to more productive businesses, provided that they are able to absorb them fully' (Oviedo *et al.* 2009: 33). While the rhetoric emphasises the 'formalisation' of informal firms, it seems that the choice of words here is misleading. If informal firms cannot survive formalisation, and instead of formalisation the aim is to shift their capital and labour into formal firms, 'formalisation' might as well be replaced by 'elimination of informal economic activity'. Even if the aim is to effectively move the labour and capital to the formal economy, the policy recommendations may encourage governments to clamp down on the informal economy. While the rhetoric focuses on encouraging 'a voluntary accommodation between private enterprise and the state' and 'creating a social contract between entrepreneurs and state' (Kenyon 2007:2), some examples of government policy inspired by this approach indicate that more drastic measures are often used to portray a 'better investment climate'. This point is further elaborated in the following chapter.

The market-based approach is characterised by the equation of people in the informal economy with entrepreneurs. However, as argued above, research shows that the informal economy comprises myriad employee-employer relations. What effect does policy planning that emphasises self-employment have on informal wage labourers? Even though the problems informal workers encounter, such as economic, social and political vulnerability and uncertainty, are mentioned (Oviedo *et al.* 2009:19), these issues are not addressed beyond the assumption that formalisation will solve them. There is a contradiction here, since it is also argued that employment-protection legislation has a negative effect on formal employment, and that formalisation should be encouraged by reducing labour regulations because this will increase formal employment. 'Reducing firing costs [has] increased worker turnover, suggesting that firms can more easily adjust their labour force according to the current economic environment' (Oviedo et al. 2009:26). This raises a question about the priorities of this strategy. According to the World Bank (2004:156), 'an investment climate that benefits all members of the society looks beyond the protection of existing jobs and confronts the challenge of creating opportunities for those in the informal economy.' If formalisation requires compromising workers' rights in the formal economy, the question arises whether it also compromises the motivation of workers to formalise? Put another way, if the informal economy is seen in such negative terms, is lowering the formal economy to the same level a viable solution? What is clear is that the priority of the market-based approach is promoting economic growth, but the social aspects of development are not properly assessed. This leads to a question of who profits from the planned economic growth. The assumption, of course, is that the welfare of the entire society will improve (World Bank 2004). The problem is that this would also require that governance practices are implemented, otherwise economic benefits will only be dealt to the elites. This point is further discussed below in the section on the state and the informal economy. Another critique of the assumption that market liberalisation will bring economic development by encouraging formalisation is that it ignores all the theories of imperialism and exploitation (Bromley 2004).

Some forms of informality may be encouraged while others are discouraged, and rhetoric may play a significant part in this. 'Bilateral aid agencies, regional development banks and non-governmental agencies have for the last couple of decades given support to informal economic activities, though not necessarily under that label.' These kinds of development projects have emphasised 'credit schemes, support to micro-enterprises, the importance of home based enterprises and small and medium enterprises' (Hansen and Vaa 2004:17). This reveals another difficulty with the development discourse relating to informality: not only is 'informality' used to mean different things, but also different terms can be used to mean informality. If a certain discourse is using informality as a concept with negative value, it can still support certain forms of informality by using different terms to legitimate them.

Rights-based approach

Since informalisation is largely driven by global processes, it would be unrealistic to assume that local policy-making could encourage formalisation in sufficient measure to counter the current trend towards informalisation. Neither is formalisation even advocated as a universal solution to the problems facing the informal economy. 'The experiences indicate that no simple rule exists that increasing or decreasing "formalisation" necessarily improves or worsens the well-being of the poor or welfare of the society at large' (Guha-Khasnobis et al. 2006:9). Instead of pursuing a universal solution, a more context-specific approach – one that also acknowledges the benefits of informality and relies on increased research and the opinions of those in informal economy – is recommended (Chen 2005). Informal employment is seen as 'a widespread feature of today's global economy that needs to be upgraded: the goal is to reduce the costs and increase the benefits of working informally' (Chen 2005:30-1).

Chen (2005) points to two shortcomings in the debate regarding formalisation. First, formalisation can be used to mean different things. For many policy-makers, formalisation means registering a business and complying with taxation regimes, whereas for people in the informal economy the focus would be on the benefits, 'including enforceable commercial contracts; legal ownership of their place of business and means of production; tax breaks and incentive packages to increase their competitiveness; membership in trade associations; and statutory social protection' (Chen 2005:30). Second, it is not clear that most bureaucracies could handle large-scale formalisation. There would be difficulties with the registration process as well as with offering the benefits of formal operation. It is also unclear whether the economy could provide so many formal jobs.

The policy recommendations of WIEGO address a wide range of issues within the informal economy. Promotion of informal enterprises in order to increase their productivity should be aided by providing them with access to services such as microfinance. Informal jobs should be improved by extending to informal work situations the legislation that currently covers only formal jobs. If existing social protection schemes cannot be extended to the informal economy, alternative schemes should be developed. One main agenda item is promoting the voice of informal workers by improving their ability to organise collectively and participate in political decision-making (Chen 2003:8). If we return to the rights-based contextualisation of the informal economy, we see that people in the informal economy are viewed as integrated economically but excluded politically and socially from the wider society. A key issue thus becomes political and social integration by encouraging the self-organising possibilities for people in informal economy. One way to improve the position of informals is by building cooperatives. There are several examples of how, for example, cooperatives of waste-pickers have improved the economic and social conditions of their members (Chikarmane and Narayan 2005, Medina 2005). Cooperatives that are initially organised as economic associations may also address social and political issues as well and give legitimacy to their members.

Informal workers' organisations are also building alliances with other social movements, including trade unions. The international labour movement is increasingly seeing the value of organising informal workers (Lindell 2008, ITUC 2010). ILO is encouraging trade union activities in the informal economy, and within academic literature there is an emerging discussion about the possibilities for trade unions to organise in the informal economy (Andrae and Backman 2010, Jimu 2010). This debate is also facilitated by the efforts of WIEGO to bring together researchers and activists working with issues relating to the informal economy and trade unionists. Arguably, trade unions struggling with decreasing memberships due to informalisation can increase their legitimacy by organising across a broader membership base that includes informal workers. Simultaneously, informal associations can gain legitimacy and official recognition by forming links with trade unions (Gallin 2001).

Although people in the informal economy are increasingly organising themselves (Lindell 2010), these organisations often still suffer because their members lack time and resources and adequate leadership skills, and because they face conflicting interests and have to deal with unhelpful or hostile political systems (Devas 2004:190). Addressing these issues is a key priority for the rights-based approach. Policies need to facilitate the right of association and extending the right to trade union membership beyond people with formal labour contracts.

6. Policy impacts: illustrations from Sub-Saharan Africa

The relationship between state and the informal economy is very complex, and no universal generalisations should be made. State attitudes can vary among different levels of government, as well as temporally and spatially. Attitudes may also be different towards specific groups within the informal economy (Lindell 2010). The aim here is to tie the above discussion of different conceptions of informality into a brief analysis of how they affect state policies.

The older dualistic conception that regarded the informal sector as a passing phenomenon affected urban planning in sub-Saharan Africa (Mitullah 2004, Potts 2008). Informality was regarded by definition as outside the planned environment, and was therefore largely disregarded. This also applies to policy-making: many by-laws concerning the informal economy are simply outdated, precisely because informality and planning have not been regarded as belonging to the same sphere (Mitullah 2004). Government attitudes have ranged from appreciating the poverty-alleviating potential of the informal economy, through ambivalence, to hostility. It must be emphasised that these views have often been contested within state governance as well. Some politicians, for instance, may defend informal workers in an attempt to win their votes in a coming election (Larmer and Fraser 2007, Lindell 2010). These sorts of issues can contribute to political uncertainty for those in the informal economy. Politicians do not generally regard the informal economy as a high priority, and attitudes towards it are easily swayed by other factors. Recent studies suggest a current trend towards hostility that is often legitimated by portraying informals as criminals, or blaming them for taking up public space and causing congestion and the spread of disease (Potts 2008, Brown and Lyons 2010).

Governments also increasingly see the informal economy as an obstacle to the interests of the elites and as discouraging international investment. This development can be viewed as being driven by an alliance between ruling parties and foreign capital (Larmer and Fraser 2007, Potts 2008). Where informality is viewed as a sign of a poor investment climate, offensives against informal workers maybe encouraged, with drastic effects on the livelihoods of the urban poor. In Ghana, the official government line has been to support informal enterprises because of their poverty-alleviating effects. However, the Ghana Railway Company, with some support from local government, has launched 'clean-ups' of vendors from railway stations in order to please international investors (Palmer 2004:80). The reason is that vendors make the stations seem less modern and compete with formal market developments at stations. Evictions of street vendors are often linked to the promotion of urban areas as modern to foreign visitors, for example, in the context of international events (Lindell, Hedman and Verboomen 2010).

A similar example can be found in Zambia, where changes in government attitudes reflect the linkages between international economic processes and developments in the informal economy. During the early 1990s, the president defended street vendors against aggression from Lusaka City Council. Within a few years, the president's attitude had changed drastically. In 1997, a planned process of formalisation made vending unprofitable by requiring increased expenditures. This process was much more effective and carefully planned than earlier harassment by local government (Potts 2008, Hansen 2010). Potts (2008:159) identifies foreign investment, free market principles and new shopping malls as being at the heart of this process. Modern shopping malls built with foreign capital were facing competition from informal street vendors, so government got rid of the vendors. These examples illustrate how global and local processes and changes in the formal economy affect the informal economy. 'In popular representations in Zambia, "freeing the market" has almost come to mean opening it up to external rather than local participation' (Hansen 2010:15). As a result, the livelihoods of thousands of informal vendors have been lost. This is an extreme example of the contradictory results of a market-driven formalisation process. What it shows is that the rhetoric of voluntary accommodation between informal enterprise and state is not always that simple in practice.

Looking at the state-informal interactions highlights another shortcoming in the market-based approach. In focusing on the economic aspects of the informal economy, this approach seems – at least to an extent – to be based on the assumption that economic growth will benefit the entire society. However, we should be more cautious about expecting too much from government. Foreign investment often only benefits elites unless good governance practices are in place and as much as 80 per cent of foreign investment may flow back as capital flight (Ndikumana and Boyce 2003).

In the Zambian case, the economic growth since the late 1990s mainly stemming from the rise in copper prices has not been able to alleviate poverty (Larmer and Fraser 2007). One result is the emergence of a populist Patriotic Front (PF) party led by Michael Sata, who 'intimates that "power" consists of a corrupt alliance between domestic political and business networks and a set of international sponsors (including foreign businesses, foreign states, and international financial institutions)' (Larmer and Fraser 2007:613). Sata's election success in 2006 was largely due to his ability to express the grievances related to unequal economic growth and urban poverty.

The relationship between state and informal economy is affected not only by the power structures of the state. People in the informal economy are also capable of affecting policy-making. While informals can try to hide from the state, they may also seek visibility and recognition. Increasingly, emerging informal economy organisations are using their collective voice to challenge criminalising state discourses and to express their grievances (Lindell 2010).

Not only are people in the informal economy organising locally and building alliances with trade unions, but some organisations are also globalising (Mitullah 2010). Examples of this are WIEGO, StreetNet and SEWA (Self-Employed Women's Association). These developments remind us that people in the informal economy should not be seen as apolitical or passive. Moreover, the atomising discourses that focus on the individual agency of informals as entrepreneurs should be contrasted with these examples of collective organising.

Through collective organising, people in the informal economy have an opportunity to make their voices heard and to bring up the issues they see as important. One of the key questions this paper has raised is what influences the different approaches to promoting formalisation, and who is supposed to gain by formalisation. I want to argue that by promoting democratic self-organising, it is possible to promote more participatory development policies that are more likely to have a positive effect on people earning their living in the informal economy. Furthermore, this approach can help to address decent work deficits and other issues that cannot be measured by economic data (Ahn 2008).

7. Conclusion

The aim of this paper has been to draw attention to how the informal economy can be portrayed in different ways, and how this can lead to different focal points and recommendations for intervention. Much past research focused on evaluating the potential for economic development, neglecting the political and social aspects of informality. However, there is an emerging strand in the literature that dwells on the political and social aspects of the informal economy. An examination of this literature reveals that we have reason to be critical of the market-based approach. Emphasis on economic aspects of informality may yield a simplified and negative picture that can lead to policy suggestions with undesired effects for a large proportion of people in the informal economy. As the example of Zambia shows, it is dangerous to portray the informal economy in such negative terms. Where informality is seen as harming the investment climate, the easiest course of action for a weak state is initiating offensives against the informal economy to 'hide' it from foreign investment interests. Criminalising state discourses are a massive problem for people in the informal economy. Portraying the informal economy in such negative terms is counterproductive to solving this problem.

A focus on economic aspects can easily lead to a conception of the informal economy as being not only an 'outlaw', but also as being unregulated or chaotic. This is important, because the failure of urban development projects often arises from 'their lack of prior consideration of the prevailing legal and institutional frameworks' (Hansen and Vaa 2004: 19). Policy recommendations rarely acknowledge the complexity of the informal regulations and institutions that may be at work in the informal economy. A market-based approach focused on economic aspects depoliticises the issue of informality. The political aspects are not simply ignored, but their existence is almost denied. This can also be linked to a broader postcolonial critique of development practices, according to which 'much of the theory and praxis of development, including some development studies, geography, and politics seems unable to break from its colonial past' (Mercer, Mohan and Power 2003: 423). Interventions are often based on top-down approaches that ignore or deny the agency of Africans, and the Western model is seen as the only possible end goal of development (Legg and McFarlane 2008). The informal economy is thought of as a bad version of the formal economy, and is analysed based on what it lacks in relation to the formal, not on what it can contribute.

Alternative voices are appearing that embrace the possibilities of urban informality. These approaches challenge the Western-centrism of development models, promoting a new kind of urban model that may be arising from informality (Mbembe and Nuttall 2008). Cross and Morales are critical of how some market-based development models aim to 'lower' the formal sector to the level of the informal, or how others aim to lift the informal to the level of the formal. They suggest instead 'that policy makers create ways in which distinct systems can intersect while existing side to side' (2007:10). The alternative discourses that promote a more positive image of the informal economy are countering criminalising state discourses. Collective organising can have a positive impact by allowing the voice of the people in the informal economy to be heard and by promoting these alternative discourses (Lindell 2010). Organising around a collective identity as workers can also have the positive effect of giving legitimacy to informal livelihoods (Chikarmane and Narayan 2005).

Another reason the market-based approach should be treated with caution is because there may be motives besides poverty reduction behind its rhetoric. This approach serves the interests of capital from the developed world by aiming to create a better investment climate. This is not to say that a better investment climate would conflict with viable poverty-reduction strategies – on the contrary, foreign direct investment can be crucial in development. However, the question is whose interest is prioritised and who is expected to profit. The fact that informal workers of formal firms are ignored suggests that worker's rights are sacrificed in the interests of economic development, as labour regulations are seen to hinder formalisation. By focusing on those sections of the informal economy in competition with foreign investment but not on the informal workforce used by formal firms, the market-based approach can be used to portray the informal economy in a specific way in order to serve the interests of global capital as opposed to labour.

Bibliography

Ahn, P-S. (2008) 'Organising as a catalyst for promoting decent work in the informal economy in South Asia', *Indian Journal of Labour Economics*, 51(4).

Andrae, G. and B. Beckman (2010) 'Alliances across the Formal-Informal Divide: South African Debates and Nigerian Experiences', in I. Lindell (ed.), *Africa's Informal Workers: Collective Agency, Alliances and Transnational Organizing in Urban Africa*, London: Zed Books.

Baah-Boateng, W. (2003) 'Poverty Alleviation through Social Dialogue: The Role of Trade Unions in Ghana' in M. Mwamadzingo and D. Saleshando (eds), *Trade Unions and Poverty Alleviation in Africa*, Geneva: ILO Bureau for Workers' Activities.

Batini, N., Y-B. Kim, P. Levine and E. Lotti (2010) 'Informal Labor and Credit Markets: A survey', IMF Working Paper WP/10/42, Washington DC: IMF.

Bhowmik, S.K. (2005) 'Street Vendors in Asia: A Review', *Economic and Political Weekly*, 28.

Bromley, R. (2004) 'Power, Property and Poverty: Why De Soto's "Mystery of Capital" cannot be solved', in A. Roy and N. Alsayyad (eds), *Urban Informality: Transnational Perspectives from the Middle East, Latin America, and South Asia,* Lanham/Boulder/New York/Toronto/Oxford: Lexington Books.

Brown, A. and M. Lyons (2010) 'Seen But Not Heard: Urban Voice and Citizenship for Street Traders', in I. Lindell (ed.), *Africa's Informal Workers: Collective Agency, Alliances and Transnational Organizing in Urban Africa,* London: Zed Books.

Carr, M. and M.A. Chen (2002) Globalization and the Informal Economy: How Global Trade and Investment Impact on the Working Poor, Working Paper on the Informal Economy, Geneva: Employment Sector, International Labour Office.

Chen, M., R. Jhabvala and F. Lund (2002) 'Supporting Workers in the Informal Economy: A Policy Framework', Geneva: Employment Section, International Labour Office.

Chen, M. (2003). 'Rethinking the Informal Economy', Ssminar paper, WIEGO, vol. 531.

Chen, M. (2005). 'The Business Environment and the Informal Economy: Creating Conditions for Poverty Reduction', Draft Paper for Committee of Donor Agencies for Small Enterprise Development Conference on Reforming the Business Environment, Cairo.

Chen, M. (2006) 'Rethinking the Informal Economy: Linkages with the Formal Economy and the Formal Regulatory Environment', in B. Gula-Khasnobis, R. Kanbur and E. Ostrom (eds), *Linking the Formal and Informal Economy: Concepts and Policies,* Oxford: Oxford University Press.

Chikarmane, P. and L. Narayan (2005) *Organising the Unorganised: A Case Study of the Kagad Kach Patra Kashtakari Panchayat (Trade Union of Wastepickers),* WIEGO.

Cross, J. and A. Morales (eds), (2007) *Street Entrepreneurs: People, Place and Politics in Local and Global Perspective,* London/New York: Routledge.

Davies, R. (1979) 'Informal Sector or Subordinate Mode of Production? A Model' in R. Bromley and C. Gerry (eds), *Casual Work and Poverty in Third World Cities,* New York: Wiley.

De Soto, H. (1989) *The Other Path,* New York: Harper and Row.

Devas, N. (ed.) (2004) *Urban Governance, Voice and Poverty in the Developing World,* London: Earthscan.

Division for the Advancement of Women (DAW) (1999) *1999 Survey on the Role of Women in Development: Globalization, Gender and Work.* New York: United Nations.

Fernandez-Kelly, P. (2006) 'Introduction' in P. Fernandez Kelly and J. Shefner (eds), *Out of the Shadows: Political Action and the Informal Economy in Latin America,* University Park PA: Penn State University Press.

Gallin, D. (2001) 'Propositions on Trade Unions and Informal Employment in Times of Globalization', *Antipode,* 33(3): 531–49.

Gula-Khasnobis, B., R. Kanbur and E. Ostrom (2006) 'Beyond Formality and Informality', in B. Gula-Khasnobis, R. Kanbur and E. Ostrom (eds), *Linking the Formal and Informal Economy: Concepts and Policies,* Oxford: Oxford University Press

Hansen, K. (2010), 'Changing Youth Dynamics in Lusaka's Informal Economy in the Context of Economic Liberalization', *African Studies Quarterly,* 11(2-3).

Hansen, K., and M. Vaa (eds) (2004), *Reconsidering Informality: Perspectives from Urban Africa*, Uppsala: Nordic Africa Institute.

Hart, K. (2008) 'Between Bureacracy and the People: A political history of informality', DIIS Working Paper no 2008/27, Copenhagen: Danish Institute for International Studies.

Hart, K. (1973) 'Informal Income Opportunities and Urban Employment in Ghana', *Journal of Modern African Studies*, 11(1).

ILO (2007) 'For Debate and Guidance, The Informal Economy', Geneva: International Labour Organisation.

ILO (2002) 'Decent Work and the Informal Economy', International Labour Conference, 90th session, Geneva: International Labour Organisation.

ILO (1995) *International conference of labour statisticians.* World Labour Report. Geneva: International Labour Organisation.

ILO (1991), The dilemma of the informal sector, Report of the Director-General, International Labour Conference, 78th Session, Geneva.

ILO (1972) *Employment, Incomes and Equality: A Strategy for Increasing Productive Employment in Kenya*, Geneva: International Labour Organisation.

ITUC (2010) Second World Congress: 'Resolution on Organising', ITUC.

Jimu, I.M. (2010) 'Self-Organized Informal Workers and Trade Union Initiatives in Malawi: Process, Challenges and Directions of Organizing the Informal Economy', in I. Lindell (ed.), *Africa's Informal Workers: Collective Agency, Alliances and Transnational Organizing in Urban Africa,* London: Zed Books.

Kenyon, T. (2007) A Framework for Thinking about Enterprise Formalization Policies in Developing Countries, Policy Research Working Paper 4235, Washington DC: World Bank

Klein, N. (2000) *No logo: Taking aim at the brand bullies*, Toronto: Knopf Canada.

Larmer, M. and A. Fraser (2007) 'Of Cabbages and King Cobra: Populist Politics and Zambia's 2006 Election', *African Affairs*, 106: 425.

Legg, S. and C. McFarlane (2008) 'Ordinary Urban Spaces: Between postcolonialism and development', *Environment and Planning,* 40: 6–14.

Lindell, I. (2008) 'Building Alliances Between Formal and Informal Workers: Experiences from Africa', in A. Bieler, I. Lindberg and D. Pillay (eds) *La-*

bour and the Challenges of Globalization: What Prospects for Transnational Unity?*, London: Pluto Press.

Lindell, I. (2010) 'The Changing Politics of Informality: Collective Organizing, Alliances and Scales of Engagement', in I. Lindell (ed.), *Africa's Informal Workers: Collective Agency, Alliances and Transnational Organizing in Urban Africa*, London and Uppsala: Zed Books and Nordic Africa Institute.

Lindell, I., M. Hedman and K-N. Verboomen (2010) The World Cup 2010 and the urban poor: 'World class cities' for all? Policy Note 2010/5, Uppsala: Nordic Africa Institute.

Loayza, N., and J. Rigolini (2006) Informality Trends and Cycles, Policy Research Working Paper 4078, Washington DC: World Bank.

Mbembe, A., and S. Nuttall (2008), 'Introduction: Afropolis', in S. Nuttall and A. Mbembe (eds), *Johannesburg: The Elusive Metropolis*, Durham NC: Duke University Press.

Medina, M. (2005). Waste Picker Cooperatives in Developing Countries, Paper prepared for WIEGO/Cornell/SEWA Conference on Membership-Based Organizations of the Poor, Ahmedabad, India.

Mercer, C., G. Mohan and M. Power (2003) 'Towards a critical political geography of African development', *Geoforum*, 34: 419–36.

Merk, J. (2008), *The Structural Crisis of Labour Flexibility: Strategies and Prospects for Transnational Labour Organising in the Garment and Sportswear Industries*, Amsterdam: Clean Clothes Campaign.

Mitullah, W.V. (2004), 'A Review of Street Trade in Africa', WIEGO/Harvard University.

Ndikumana, L., and J.K. Boyce (2003) 'Public Debts and Private Assets: Explaining Capital Flight from Sub-Saharan African Countries', *World Development*, 31(1).

Oviedo, A.M., M.R. Thomas and K. Karakurum-Özdemir (2009) 'Economic informality – Causes, costs, and policies: A literature survey', World Bank Working Paper no. 167, Washington DC: World Bank.

Palmer, R. (2004) 'The Informal Economy in Sub-Saharan Africa: Unresolved Issues of Concept, Character and Measurement', Occasional Papers No. 98. Centre of African Studies, University of Edinburgh.

Potts, D. (2008) 'The urban informal sector in sub-Saharan Africa: From bad to good (and back again?)', *Development Southern Africa*, 25(2): 151–67.

Roy, A. (2005). 'Urban Informality: Toward an Epistemology of Planning', *Journal of the American Planning Association*, 71(2):147–58.

Roy, A. and N. Alsayyad (eds) (2004) *Urban Informality: Transnational Perspectives from the Middle East, Latin America, and South Asia*, Lanham/Boulder/New York/Toronto/Oxford: Lexington Books.

Wilson, D.C., C. Velis and C. Cheeseman (2006), 'Role of informal sector recycling in waste management in developing countries', *Habitat International*, 30(4).

World Bank (2004) *World Development Report 2005: A Better Investment Climate for Everyone*, Washington DC: World Bank and Oxford University Press.

About the Author

Antti Vainio has a bachelor's degree from the University of Brighton and a master's degree from the Department of Human Geography, Stockholm University. He has been a research assistant at the Nordic Africa Institute (2011–12) and is currently working in the trade union movement. His research interests include union organising for vulnerable workers and labour internationalism.